Contents

SUPREME COURT ADVOCATES ON RECORD ASSOCIATION VS UNION OF INDIA 1993- CHECK ON UNTETHERED EXECUTIVE INFLUENCE

VOLUME 2, ISSUE 1 OF BRILLOPEDA

SHAMBHVI AGARWAL

Preface

"Start writing, no matter what. The water does not flow until the faucet is turned on".

-Louis L'Amour

Hundreds of students and professors are contributing their work to Brillopedia, we are here to provide ample information about Law and Contemporary issues. Our aim is to provide a platform for today's generation to express their views and ideas on law and contemporary law.

Author

Shambhvi Agarwal

Publication

This research paper is published in volume 2, issue 1 of Brillopedia

CHAPTER ONE

ABSTRACT

6th October 1993 holds a significant position in the pages of history for the Indian Judiciary. On this fine day, a Landmark Judgement was delivered by the constitutional bench Ratnavel Pandian, A.M. Ahmadi, Kuldip Singh, J.S. Verma, M.M. Punchhi, Yogeshwar Dayal, G.N. Ray, Dr. A.S. Anand, S.P. Bharuchaon the case of Supreme Court Advocates onRecord Association vs. Union of India[1].

In the light of this case, the paper grants deep insight intohow judicial independence is fundamental for the healthy survival of democracy. Firstly, the paper highlights a few judicial interpretations which form the foundation or background of the case. The paper further offers a brief explanation of the facts, and then it highlights the issues raised. It then deliberates the clashing arguments presented by the petitioners and the respondents. The paper further expounds on what all laws and doctrines have applied to this landmark judgment, beginning with Articles 124, 217, and 50 of the Indian Constitution; and Doctrine of Rule of Law, Separation of Powers, and Checks and Balances. Also, the paper presents the highlights of the judgment. Towards the end, the paper presents a proper conclusion and critical analysis of the whole judgment.

The expected outcomes of this paper are-

1. Accentuating the true essence of the term 'consultation' in Articles 124 and 217 of the Indian Constitution.
2. Underlining theimportance of participatory consultative procedure for the appointment of judges of Supreme Court and High Courts.
3. Critically addressing and scrutinizing the judgment.

Keywords- Supreme Court Advocates on Record Association vs Union of India, Article 124, Article 217, Appointment, Consultation, Rule of Law,

Separation of Powers, Checks and Balances, Critical Analysis.

[1]Supreme Court Advocates on Record Association v. Union of India, AIR 1994 SC 868

CHAPTER TWO

INTRODUCTION

The landmark case of Supreme Court Advocates on Record Association vs. Union of India is famously known as the 'Second Judge Transfer Case'. This case isfounded on the freedom of the judiciary as the fragment of the basic structure of the Constitution under the light of Article 124 of the Indian Constitution. The case highlighted that Dicey's 'Rule of Law' can only be embraced when the principle of separation of power which forms a part of the Indian Constitution and talks about 'separation of judiciary from the executive', is followed. The survival of the concept of rule of law is essential for the preservation of the democratic system. The case was ruled on 6th October 1993. After the judgment collegium system was implemented in the selection of judges of Supreme Court and High Courts.

CHAPTER THREE

BACKGROUND

Article 124, of the Indian Constitution, talks about the establishment and constitution of the Supreme Court but stands silent on the concrete procedure of the appointment of judges. This silence led to a major clash between the executive and the judiciary. Article 124 clause 2 states that the President has the power to appoint the Judge of the Supreme court, but here it is mentioned that he can exercise his power after the 'consultation' from Chief Justice of India and the Judges of the Supreme Court. Here the eye of the storm is the term 'consultation'.

The main question that was posed was whether the opinion of the executive functioning under the aid and advice of the Prime Minister and Council of Ministers, is given priority or it's the CJI's opinion. So, in the case of Union of India vs. Sankal Chand Himatlal Seth[1], based on the literal meaning of the article it was quoted that it is nowhere mentioned in Article 124 of the Indian Constitution that the opinion of the CJI is binding on the President, therefore the President cannot be said to be bounded by the opinion of CJI. Here the controversy began as the executive was given more importance than the judiciary, that too in a judicial matter.

Similarly, in the case of S.P. Gupta vs. Union of India[2],the executive was given more gravity. Here, the judgment was criticized a lot and it was said by several jurists across India that the judgment is bypassing the constitutional procedure and is not adhered to in its true letter and spirit.

In Subhash Sharma vs. Union of India case[3], it was highlighted that the appointment of the judges is not purely executive act, the constitution-makers wanted it to be a fair consultative procedure, they never wanted to leave it at the sole prerogative of the executive as Judiciary forms a part of the basic structure of the constitution and if you place vital importance in the executive, you will ultimately be hampering the independence of the judiciary. So here SC being the court of record under Article 129 of the Indian Constitution took note of the earlier judgments and having the authority to review its own judgments under Article 137 of the constitution, ordered to review the judgment of the S.P. Gupta case, and formulated a 9-judge bench. It further stated that the principle of constitutionalism should be the sole bases of granting power to the authorities and therefore the executive shall not be given unchartered authority in Article 124 as if done so, the judges will start working as the puppets of the government that is to fulfill the political desires.

Then came the case of Supreme Court Advocates on Record Association vs. Union of India 1993, wherein the collegium system was adopted.

[1]Union of India v. Sankal Chand Himatlal Seth, 1977 AIR 2328

[2]S.P. Gupta v. Union of India, AIR 1982 SC 149

[3]Subhash Sharma v. Union of India, 1991 AIR 631

CHAPTER FOUR

FACTS OF THE CASE

The eye of the storm that is, the term 'consultation' mentioned in Article 124 of the Constitution was interpreted in this case. Before 1993, primacy was granted to the opinion of the government that is Executive and its team but after 1994 the situation evolved through this case. In 1993, the Chief Justice of India got primacy in appointing judges and his team.

The matters linking to the nomination of the judges have inundated and mystified the judicial mind ever since the commencement of the constitution and the judiciary has tried solving this puzzle through judicial interpretations. The judicial interpretation tried striking asubtleequilibrium between democratic control of an essentially undemocratic institution and impartial arbitration.

The question related to what is the true essence of the term 'consultation' and who's opinion will be given primacy was first raisedin Sankal Chand vs. Union of India, where the court gave primacy to the executive's decision over the Chief Justice of India. A similar interpretation was drawn in the S.P. Gupta case. These consecutive interpretations drew criticism by several jurists across the country wherein they pointed out that these decisions are bypassing the very constitutional procedure of the country and the constitution is not followed in its letter and spirit. While deciding this case the honourable Supreme Court conferred the decisive control with the Central Government that is the executive. At this interval, a bill was presented in the parliament seeking to amend the Constitution [67th Amendment] Bill 1990in the quest to amend Articles 124(2), 217(1), 222(1), and 231(2)(a). This bill granted the authority to the president to set up National Judicial Commission. The avowed objective of this bill was to implement the 121st Law Commission Report whichsuggested that a judicial commission is to beformed to supervise the selection of the judges of Supreme Court and High Courts. But the true colours of the bill did not show up as it got lapsed due to the dissolution of the 9th Lok Sabha.

Finally, a writ petitions under Article32 of the Indian Constitution was filed seeking a review of the judgment laid inthe S.P. Gupta case by a 9-judge constitutional bench.

ISSUES RAISED

Two major issues raised were-

1. What is the importance of the term "consultation" referred to under Article 124 clause 2 of the Constitution of India?
2. Whether the opinion of the Chief Justice of India should be given primacy with regard to the appointment and selection of Judges of High Courts and the Supreme Court, as well as in the transfer of Judges from one High Court to another?

CHAPTER FIVE

ARGUMENTS BY THE PETITIONER

The petitioners through their counsels highlighted Article 50 of the Indian Constitution which states that the executive must be separate from the functioning of the judiciary as much as possible. Therefore, considering the upper hand of the executive in the selectionprocess is a strongbreach of the essence of Article 50. The meddling of the executive in judicial appointments must be minimized and CJI recommendation shall not be overlooked as the appointment of judges is a matter in relation to the judiciary. They further pointed out that since President's opinions are considered of primary importance, the same has made the CJI a passive body instead of him being an active partaker in the nominationpractice. This uninvolved status of CJI has been demonstrated to be counter-productive to the freedom of judiciary which is granted in the country. The rudimentary feature of independence of the judiciary is chokedand trapped in the vicious clutches ofexecutive dominance and the product of the same will becorrosion of a free and fair spirit of justice. This will ultimately go against the Preamble of the Indian Constitution which reflects justice as a vital and prima-facie element. At last, the petitioners pointed out that the word "consultation" must be constructed equivalent to "concurrence" in order to preserve the independence of the Judiciary.

CHAPTER SIX

ARGUMENTS BY THE RESPONDENT

On the other hand, the respondents argued that the President is an executive head and with respect to Articles 124 & 214 of the Constitution, he is granted authority by the Constitution of India to appoint judges in Supreme Court and High Courts based on the aid and advice of the Council of Ministers. The respondents referred to CJI as a mere consultant in the process. The Constitution has vested greater autonomy in the President in the appointment procedure and CJI is vested with a role to provide factual knowledge to the President regarding the consideration of the candidate for the position. This marks the end of CJI's role and after gathering the knowledge it's the President to lastly appoint whoever he considers suitable to clasp the office.

Furthermore, they stated that the executive opposing the opinion of CJI raises no question on the independence of the judiciary rather it forms a part of debate and discussion. They submitted that the independence of the judiciary is not violated. Also, the appointment of judges by an executive body will not abuse the term justice as the judge owes his confidence & commitment to the law of the land and not to the employing authority.

Further, the respondents presented their points on the transfer and removal of judges. They quoted that the tenure of the office of the judges is secured by the Constitution of India and no authority either Parliament or Executive has the capability to eliminate the judge from his positionuntil the question is of impeachment. As per the Constitution, the Parliament has no right to reduce the quantum of a judge's salary, perks,& allowances by a unanimous bill. They highlighted that the conduct of a judge of the Supreme Court or High Courts can on no occasion be deliberated in a sitting of Parliament due to the privileges granted by the Constitution.The higher judicial courts are granted the authority to decide the constitutionality of actions of the administrations of the state as well as the union government. Therefore, by the virtue of these provisions, the Parliamentof Executive can never harm judicial independence.

CHAPTER SEVEN

APPLICATION OF LAWS

1) Article 124 clause 2 of the Indian Constitution- This Article states that the appointment of the judges of the Supreme Court shall be done by the President under his hand and seal after consultation of the judges and the CJI.

2) Article 217 of the Indian Constitution- This Article states that the selection of the judges of the High Court shall be done by the President under his seal after consultation of the judges, the CJI, and the Governor of State.

3) Article 50 of the Indian Constitution- This Article talks about the separation of judiciary from the executive. It states that the State shall take steps to detach the judiciary from the executive in the public amenities of the State.

4) Doctrine of Rule of Law- Dicey's rule of law places emphasis on supremacy or predominance of legal spirit.

5) Doctrine of Separation of Power- Montesquieu's theory of separation of power is based upon the idea that each authority is vested with certain responsibilities and functions, hence it is their duty to function accordingly. One authority is not allowed to intervene in the affairs of another authority until there is a breach of constitutional provisions.

6) Doctrine of Checks and Balances- This doctrine reflects that no authority under the roof of the constitution is granted unrestricted or absolute powers. The biggest check on the authorities is the constitution itself and if one authority finds that the other is breaching the constitutional provisions, it can intervene to prevent such breach and abuse of power.

CHAPTER EIGHT

HIGHLIGHTS OF THE JUDGEMENT

In light of the issues raised the nine-judge bench overruled the judgment of the S.P. Gupta Case with a 7:2 majority.It was held that in the matter of appointment of judges of Supreme Court and the High Courts, the president is bound to act in harmony with the opinion of the CJI who would under tender his opinion on the matter after consulting his team. The opinion of the CJI was granted a greater weightage in the nomination of the candidates. The judges stateabout the 'participatoryconsultative process' wherein they mentionedthatthe executive should have the power to act as a check on the exercise of power by CJI, in order to keep the spirit of the Constitution alive.The Executive was levied with a responsibility that if it finds the decision or opinions of the CJI irrelevant, arbitrary, or malafide, then it can act as a check on the abuse of power. Collegium system [2 senior-most judges must be consulted] was adopted. As a whole, CJI's opinion was given primacy over the Executive's opinion. The court reduced the executive elements in the appointment of judges to a minimum level and therefore eliminated the political influence. This is how the judges supported the term 'consultation' over 'concurrence'. No absolute power was granted to any authority under the judgment.

CHAPTER NINE

CONCLUSION

Democracy forms the very roots of the constitution of India. This democracy imparts the term 'independence' in the system. If we talk about Judiciary under the Indian system, it works as a sentinel on the qui vive that is as a watchdog or guarding guardian. Its main function is to adjudicate the laws. They are seen upon as a source of seeking justice and fulfillment of this curtail duty rather than responsibility that is levied upon their shoulders, is only possible the judges act independently and impartially. There impartial and independent conduct can only be facilitated by keeping them away from the external pressure so that those who appear before them and the wider public can have confidence and faith that their cases will be decided fairly and in accordance with the law as justice forms the major part in the Preamble of the constitution.

The case of Supreme Court Advocates on Record Association vs. Union of India 1993,torched the independence of the judicial bodies. The judgment stands to be vital as it laid a firm foundation by overruling the past judgments wherein the supremacy of the concluding word was given to the government. Past mistakes were rectified through this judgment. The bench gave up a much more liberal and flexible interpretation of the word "Consultation". By the virtue of this judgment the government authorities cannot overlook the view and recommendation of the Chief Justice of India thereby reducing executive influence, partypoliticsand biasness, and favoritism.

CHAPTER TEN

CRITICAL ANALYSIS

- The author affirms that it was a balanced judgment wherein it was reflected that appointment of a judge is a judicial matter and therefore the Executive should have minimized say in the same. Article 50 was followed to the core.
- Judgment tried protecting the integrity and guarding the independence of the judiciary. The judgment established the fact that independence of judiciary is a basic feature of the constitution and hence the appointment of judges should not be influenced by political considerations.
- The judgment also holds a major flaw as it did not lay a concrete foundation of how CJI is going to make his decisions with regards to the selection of the candidates, this leaves a loophole due to which favoritism and biasness can still take place.
- Furthermore, a large chunk of the judgment is obiter as it holds no set references. The reference was majorly confined to the question of 'primacy of opinion' and fixation of the strength of the judges. Hence, the rest of the judgment stands to be mere obiter.

9 798886 294576

Printed by Libri Plureos GmbH in Hamburg,
Germany